BEST OF
LENNY KRAVITZ
FOR GUITAR

Management: HK Management/Howard Kaufman

Photography by Per Gustafsson

Visit our website at www.cherrylane.com

CONTENTS

Are You Gonna Go My Way

Words by Lenny Kravitz
Music by Lenny Kravitz and Craig Ross

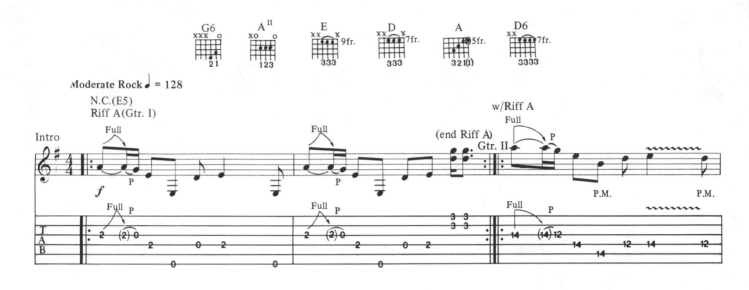

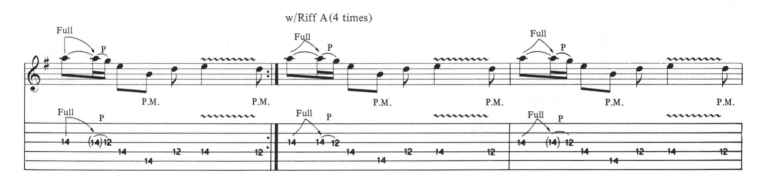

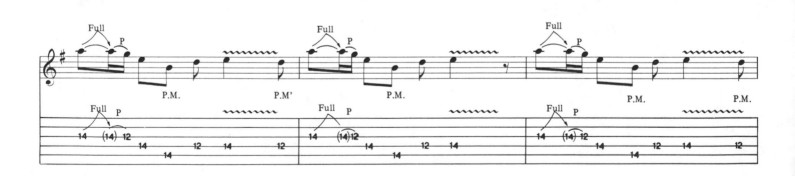

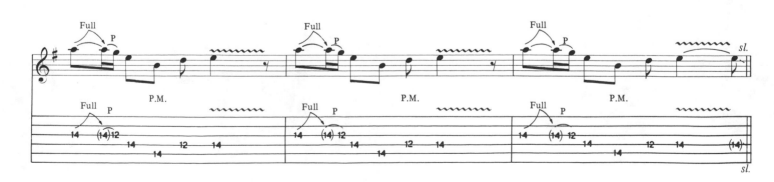

1st, 2nd Verses
w/Riff A (1st bar only) (8 times)
N.C.(E5)

1. I was born_____ long a-go. I'm the cho-sen, I'm the one.
2. *See additional lyrics*

I have come_____ to save the day. And I won't leave un-til I'm done.

(G5)

So that's why_____ you got to try. You got to breathe and have some fun.

2nd time substitute Rhy. Fill 1
(Gtr. II only)

Gtr. II
Full   P

P.M.

Full   P

(Gtr. II out)

Gtr. I   Full   P

Full   P

w/Riff A (1st bar only) (4 times)
(E5)

Though I'm not paid,_____ I play this game. And I won't stop un-til I'm done.

Rhy. Fill 1

(Gtr. II out)

5

*With one vol. knob set to zero, flick toggle
switch back and forth in specified rhythm.

Additional Lyrics

2. I don't know why we always cry.
   This we must leave and get undone.
   We must engage and rearrange.
   And turn this planet back to one.
   So tell me why we got to die
   And kill each other one by one.
   We've got to love and rub-a-dub.
   We've got to dance and be in love.
   But what I really want to know is... *etc.*

Believe

Words by Lenny Kravitz
Music by Lenny Kravitz and Henry Hirsch

Additional Lyrics

2. The Son of God is in our face,
   Offering us eternal grace.
   If you want it, you got to believe.
   'Cause being free is a state of mind.
   We'll one day leave this all behind.
   Just put your faith in God, and one day you'll see, yeah. *(To Chorus)*

3. The future's in our present hands.
   Let's reach right in. Let's understand.
   If you want it, you got to believe, yeah. *(To Chorus)*

Circus

Words and Music by Gerry DeVeaux
and Terry Britten

*Rhythm gtrs. tuned down 2 whole steps.
Chord names reflect sounding pitches.

Slowly ♩ = 84

*Tune down 2 whole steps (low to high): C F B♭ E♭ G C. All parts sound as indicated.
**T = Fret ⑥ w/thumb.

1st Verse
w/Rhy. Fig. 1 (Gtrs. I & II) (2 times)

One day while I was search-ing *Tune down as before. for what I'll nev-er find,

she walked in-to my sto-ry,

said she could change my mind.

to get a - long.— What can I do? Got to be strong.—

Fields Of Joy

Words and Music by Michael Kamen
and Hal Fredricks

*Acoustic.

1st Verse
w/Rhy. Fig. 1 and Riff A (both 5 times)

wan-der slow-ly through the fields,— slow - ly, slow - ly through the fields._____ I

touch the leaves that touch the sky.__ Just you and I,_____

____ through fields ___ of joy._____ All

Riff A
*Gtr. II

*Mellotron (flute sound) arr. for gtr.

2nd Verse
w/Rhy. Fig. 1 and Riff A (both 5 times)

trou - ble slow - ly fades a - way,____
(Ooh.____

slow - ly, slow - ly fades a -
Ooh.____

way.____

I hold your hand in - side my hand.____
Ooh.)

A -

cross the land,____ through fields_ of joy.____

The

Bridge

Gtr. III *f*

sound of mu - sic that we hear.____

The blend of col - ors in the air.____

All

cit - ies, moun - tains dis - ap - pear____ from view._

All truth_ and beau - ty near to me_ and you._

With

w/Rhy. Fig. 3 (3 times)
*B

you through_ the fields.____

With you through_ the fields.____

With

*Implied chords (next 6 bars).

w/Rhy. Fig. 2

you through_ the fields,____ the fields of joy.____
(Joy.)____

Yeah!

Rhy. Fig. 3
Gtr. III

*Full bend on 2nd string catches 3rd string, bending it up 1/2 step.

*Full bend on top 2 strings catches 3rd string, bending it up 1/4 step.

*Implied chords (next 6 bars).

Rhy. Fill 1

Fly Away

Words and Music by
Lenny Kravitz

Is There Any Love In Your Heart

Words by Lenny Kravitz
Music by Lenny Kravitz and Craig Ross

Is there an-y love in your heart?

Ooh_____ yeah!_____

31

Is there an-y love in your heart?_____ Ooh!

all the lat - est trends._____

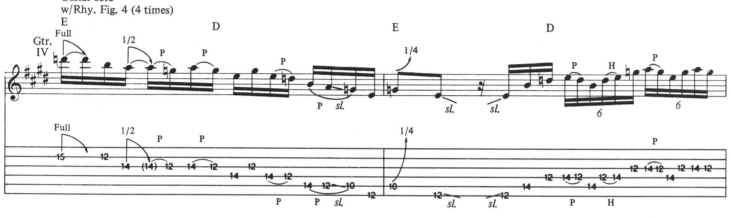

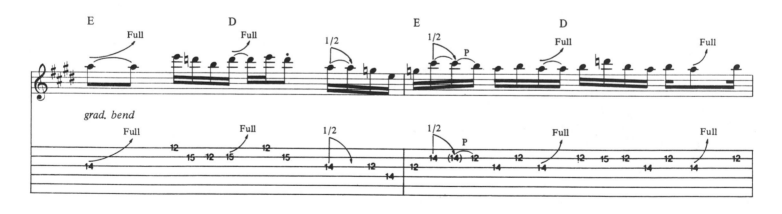

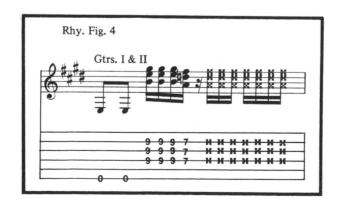

Rhy. Fig. 4

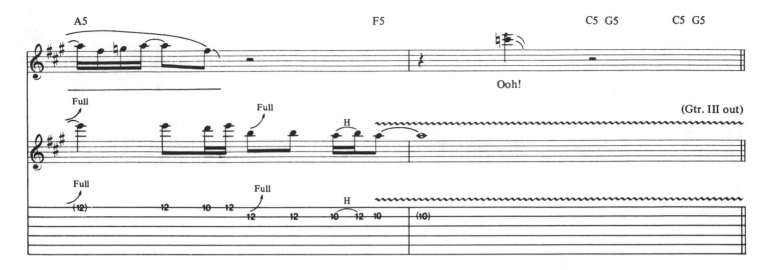

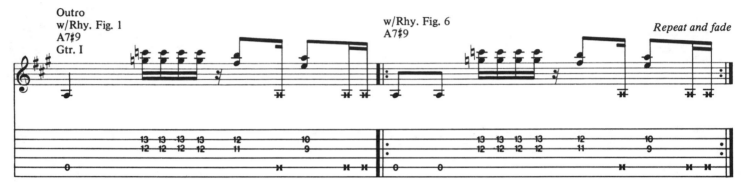

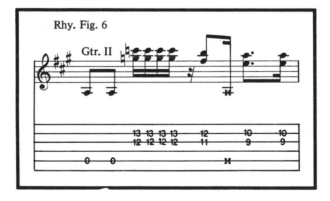

Additional Lyrics

2. Baby, baby you walk around like you own this town.
   Your whole life is a fantasy, and I'm playing the clown.
   You talk behind my back and spend up all my bread. *(To Chorus)*

3. Babe, you say I'm the only one, but you're fucking all my friends.
   Baby, all that you care about is Gucci and Mercedes Benz.
   You're just the kind that's up on all the latest trends.

It Ain't Over 'Til It's Over

Words and Music by
Lenny Kravitz

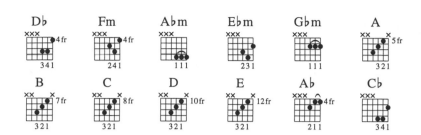

Light Funk ♩=84

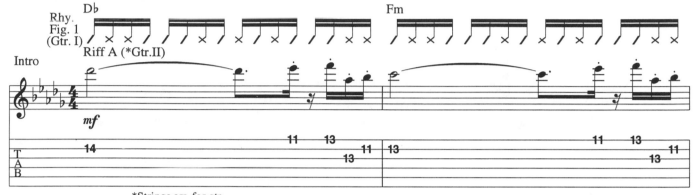

*Strings arr. for gtr.

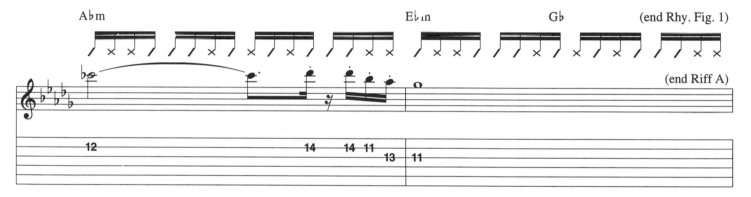

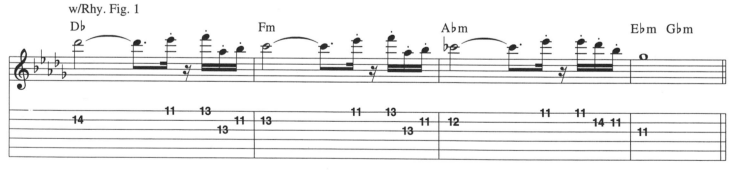

1st Verse
w/Rhy. Fig. 1 (2 times)

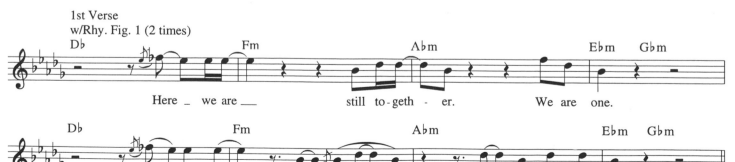

Here _ we are ___ still to-geth - er. We are one.

So _ much time _ wast - ed _____ play - ing games with love.

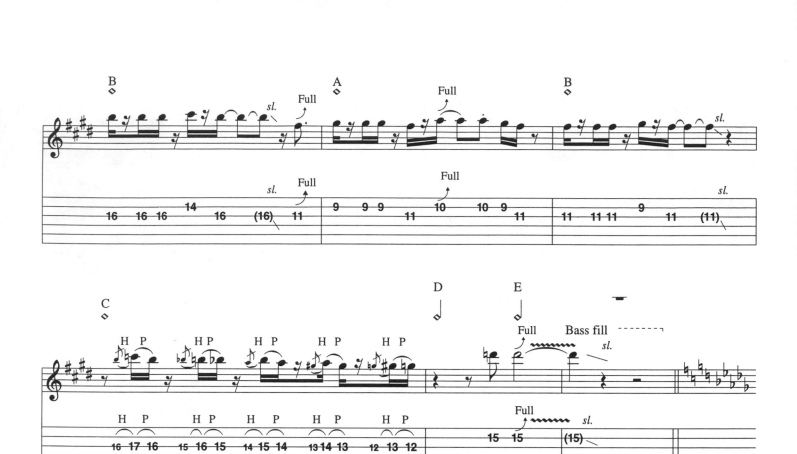

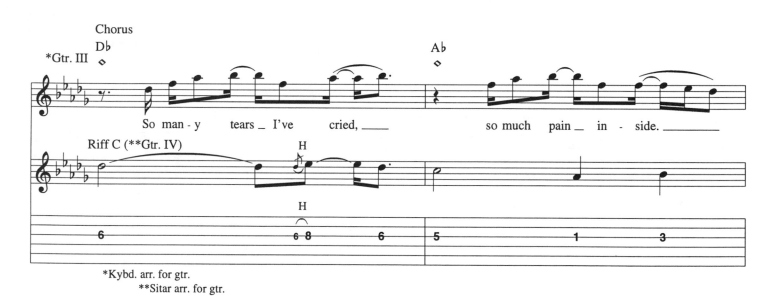

*Kybd. arr. for gtr.
**Sitar arr. for gtr.

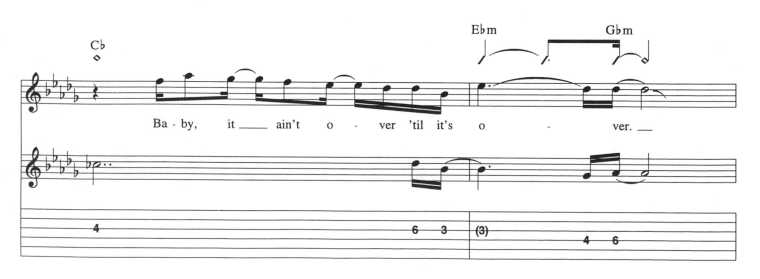

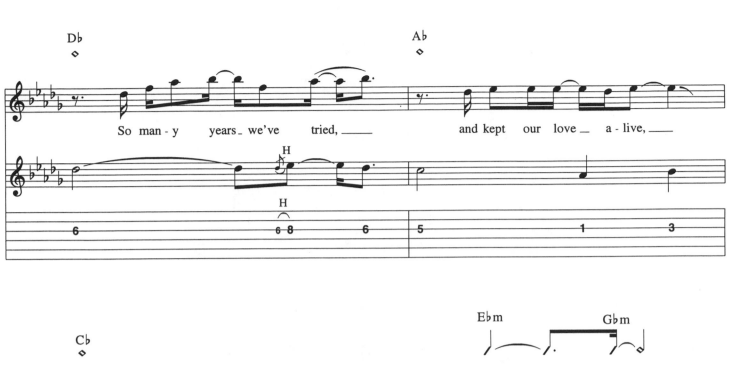

So man-y years— we've tried, _____ and kept our love _ a-live, _____

'cause ba-by, it ain't o-ver 'til it's o- ver. _____

w/Rhy. Fig. 1 (2 times) and Riffs A & C

So man-y tears _ I've cried, _____ so much pain - in - side, _____

but ba-by, it _____ ain't o-ver 'til it's o- ver. _____

w/Riff B

So _____ man-y years _ we've _ tried _____ to keep our love _ a - live,

Repeat ad lib and fade

'cause ba-by, it _____ ain't o-ver 'til it's o- ver. _____

Let Love Rule

Words and Music by
Lenny Kravitz

*1st note of this bar is tied, not struck.

*distortion on.

(continue ad lib till Outro)

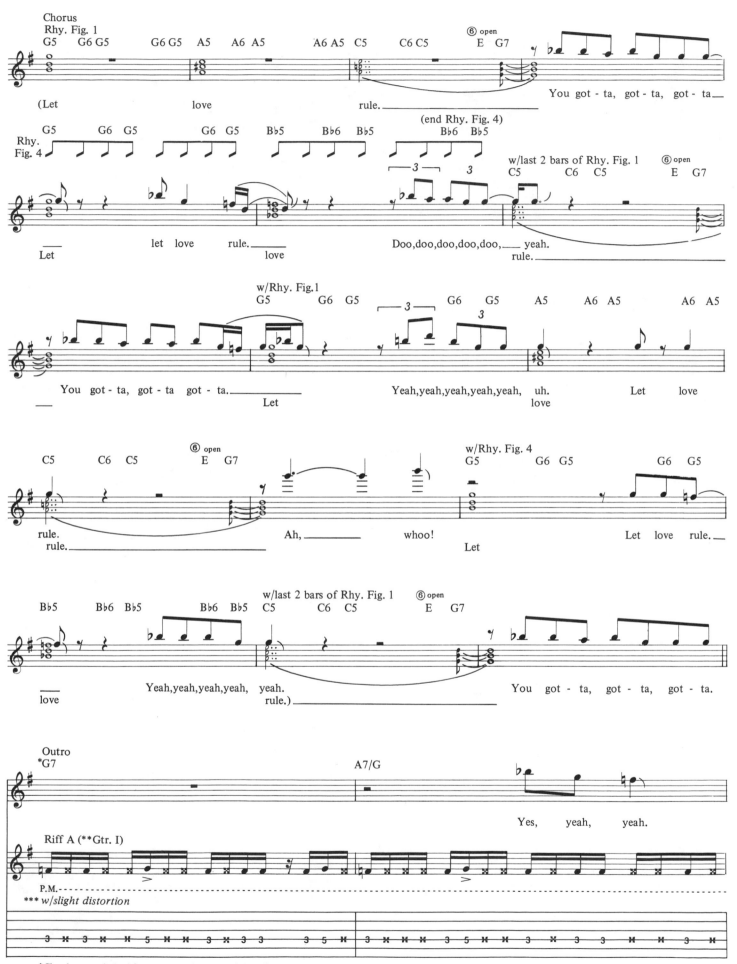

Doo-bie, doo-bie, doo-bie, doo-bie, doo, yeah,

(end Riff A)

*Play note in parentheses first time only.

semi-harm.

*w/Riff A

yeah, yeah.   You got   to, yeah.   Whee!__

*Play Riff A w/variations when recalled.

w/Fill 2

w/Riff A

You got-ta,   got-ta, got-ta, got-ta, yeah.__

w/Fill 3

Yeah, yeah, yeah, yeah, yeah, yeah.   Let love   rule.__

w/Fill 4

w/Riff A

Fill 2
Gtr. I
P.M.

Fill 3
Gtr. I
P.M.

Fill 4
Gtr. I
P.M.

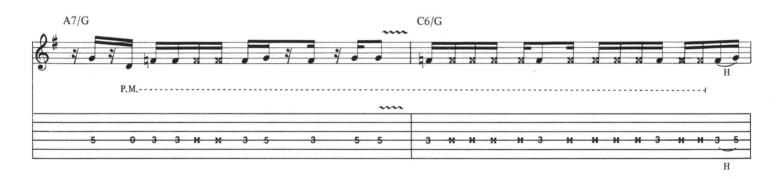

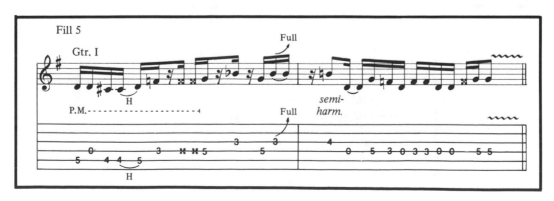

Magdalene

Words and Music by
Lenny Kravitz

*Indicated to right of slash in TAB

Mr. Cab Driver

Words and Music by
Lenny Kravitz

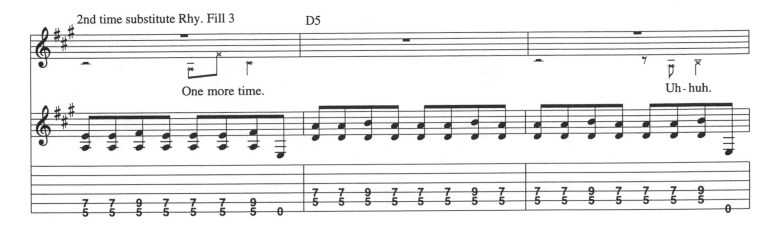

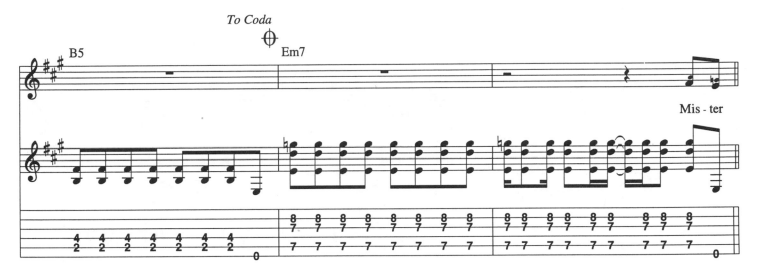

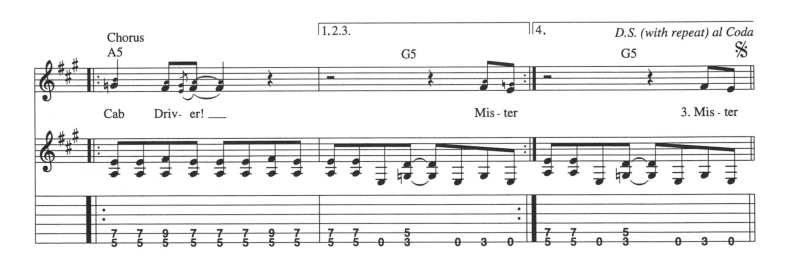

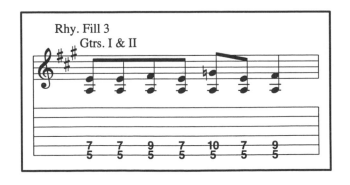

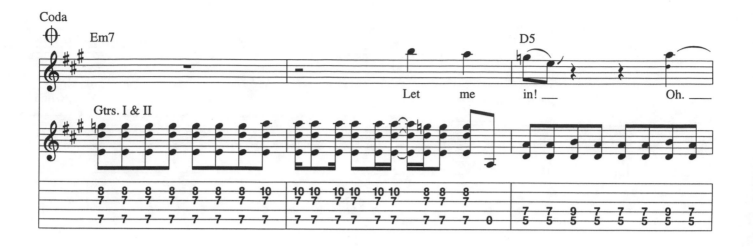

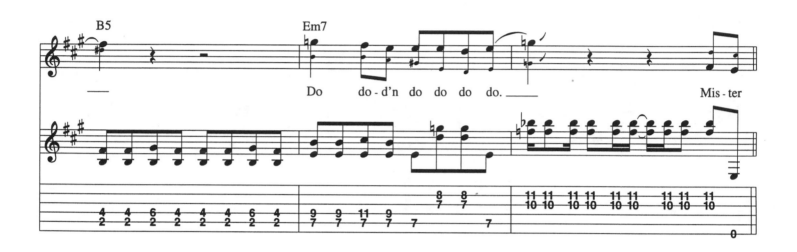

Additional Lyrics

2. Mr. Cab Driver won't stop to pick me up.
   Mr. Cab Driver I might need some help.
   Mr. Cab Driver only thinks about himself.

3. Mr. Cab Driver don't like the way I look.
   He don't like dreads. He thinks we're all crooks.
   Mr. Cab Driver reads too many storybooks.

4. Mr. Cab Driver pass me up with eyes of fire.
   Mr. Cab Driver thinks we're all 165'ers.
   Mr. Cab Driver, fuck you. I'm a surviver.

My Love

Words by Lenny Kravitz
Music by Lenny Kravitz and Craig Ross

Wan - na lose my mind____ in - side your head.__
Wan - na lose my mind____ in - side your bed.__

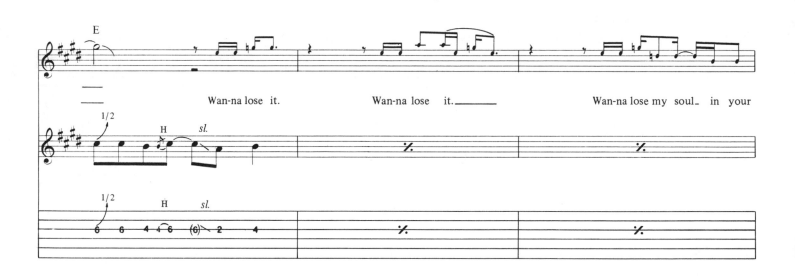

Wan-na lose it. Wan-na lose it.____ Wan-na lose my soul_ in your

2. My bed.____

Rock And Roll Is Dead

Words and Music by
Lenny Kravitz

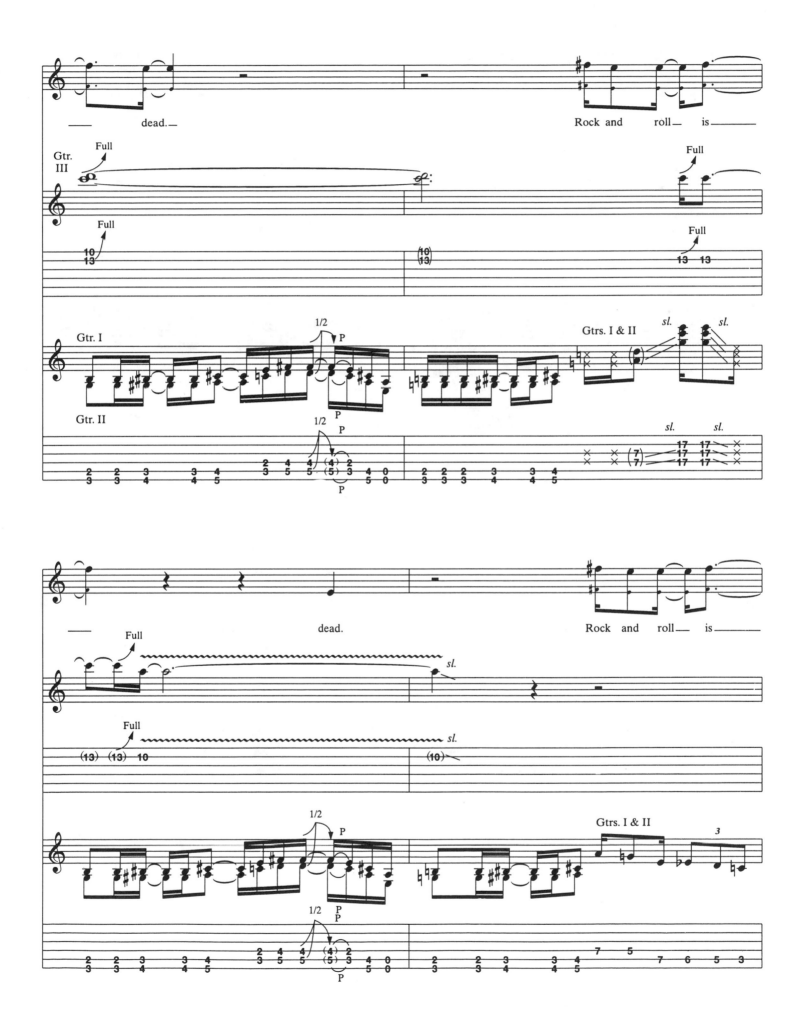

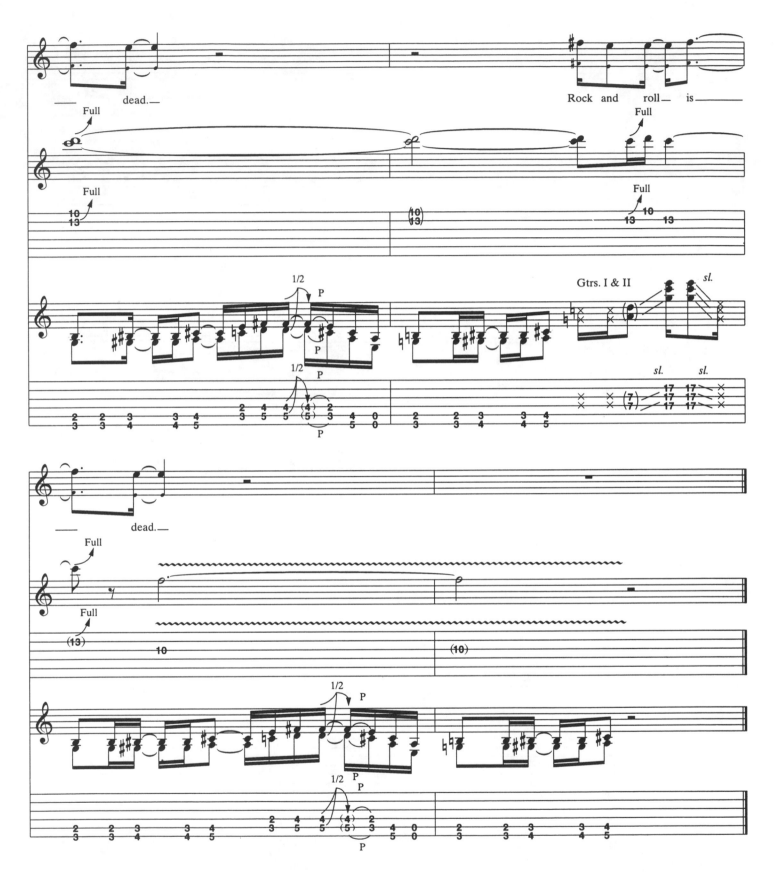

Additional Lyrics

2. You can't even sing or play an instrument
   So you just scream instead. Ooh, yeah!
   You're livin' for an image
   So you got five hundred women in your bed. Ooh, yeah!
   Rock and roll is dead.
   But it's real hard to be yourself
   When you're livin' with those demons in your head. Ooh, yeah! *(To Chorus)*

Sister

Words and Music by
Lenny Kravitz

with a man

that nev-er was _____ up to no good? ___ He look your soul ___

and he stole your on-ly heart, _____

flipped your wig ___
(end Rhy. Fig. 1)
Rhy. Fig. 2
and left a per-ma-nent scar.

don't need no more of what's ail - ing you. Just lean on your soul with

all that it takes. May God bring you back home to A - mer - i - ca, A - mer-
(all that it takes.)

i - ca, A - mer-

Fill 3 (Gtr. III)

i - ca,   hah, _____   A   -   mer   -   i - ca, ___

A   -   mer   -   i - ca. _____

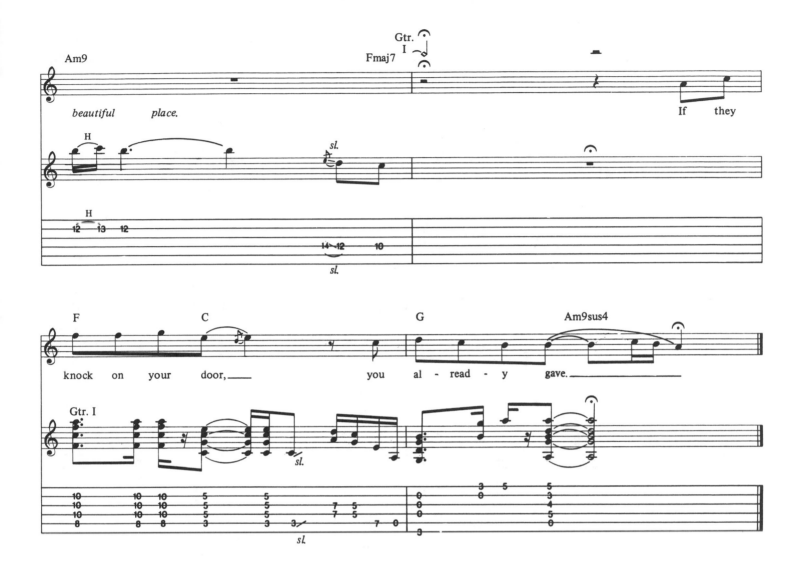

Additional Lyrics

3. Sister, sister, sister, sister, sister, it's just a test of faith.
   Your heart is pure, so the devil's in your face.
   I'll see you soon, 'cause they haven't got a case.
   And you'll be free in a beautiful place, *(etc.)*

Tunnel Vision

Words and Music by
Lenny Kravitz

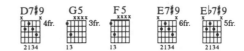

Chorus
w/Rhy. Figs. 1 & 1A (both 4 times)

I got that tun-nel vi-sion___ go-in' through my head.___

I can't help my-self,___ all I see is red.___ Tun-nel vi-sion___ go-in' through my head.__

___ Lay me down be-side___ your fly-in' bed.___

Tun-nel vi-sion___ go-in' though my head.___ I can't help my-self,___ all I see is red.___

___ Tun-nel vi-sion___ go-in' through my head.___

(Gtr. II out)

Lay me down be-side___ your fly-in' bed.

Guitar solo
*Bb/Ab   A9   D7#9   Bb7#9   A9

Gtr. IV

w/dist. & wah as filter

Gtr. I

*For next 6 bars only, chords implied by gtr. & bass.

You're My Flavor

Words and Music by
Lenny Kravitz

Additional Lyrics

2. The way you touch me.
   Somehow it takes away the pain.
   And now I'm a junkie,
   I'm runnin' 'round without a brain.
   I've got this jones deep inside me.
   And you are what I wanna do.
   You give me this feelin'.
   You always make me feel brand-new. *(To Chorus)*

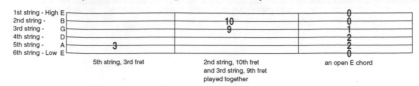

• Tablature Explanation/Notation Legend •

TABLATURE: A six-line staff that graphically represents the guitar fingerboard. By placing a number on the appropriate line, the string and the fret of any note can be indicated. For example:

1st string - High E
2nd string - B
3rd string - G
4th string - D
5th string - A
6th string - Low E

5th string, 3rd fret

2nd string, 10th fret and 3rd string, 9th fret played together

an open E chord

Definitions for Special Guitar Notation

BEND: Strike the note and bend up a half step (one fret).

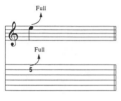

BEND: Strike the note and bend up a whole step (two frets).

BEND AND RELEASE: Strike the note and bend up a half (or whole) step, then release the bend back to the original note. All three notes are tied; only the first note is struck.

PRE-BEND: Bend the note up a half (or whole) step, then strike it.

PRE-BEND AND RELEASE: Bend the note up a half (or whole) step, strike it and release the bend back to the original note.

UNISON BEND: Strike the two notes simultaneously and bend the lower note to the pitch of the higher.

VIBRATO: Vibrate the note by rapidly bending and releasing the string with a left-hand finger.

WIDE OR EXAGGERATED VIBRATO: Vibrate the pitch to a greater degree with a left-hand finger or the tremolo bar.

SLIDE: Strike the first note and then with the same left-hand finger move up the string to the second note. The second note is not struck.

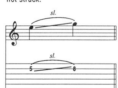

SLIDE: Same as above, except the second note is struck.

SLIDE: Slide up to the note indicated from a few frets below.

HAMMER-ON: Strike the first (lower) note, then sound the higher note with another finger by fretting it without picking.

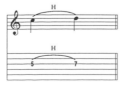

PULL-OFF: Place both fingers on the notes to be sounded. Strike the first (higher) note, then sound the lower note by pulling the finger off the higher note while keeping the lower note fretted.

TRILL: Very rapidly alternate between the note indicated and the small note shown in parentheses by hammering on and pulling off.

TAPPING: Hammer ("tap") the fret indicated with the right-hand index or middle finger and pull off to the note fretted by the left hand.

NATURAL HARMONIC: With a left-hand finger, lightly touch the string over the fret indicated, then strike it. A chime-like sound is produced.

ARTIFICIAL HARMONIC: Fret the note normally and sound the harmonic by adding the right-hand thumb edge or index finger tip to the normal pick attack.

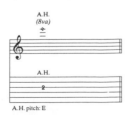

TREMOLO BAR: Drop the note by the number of steps indicated, then return to original pitch.

PALM MUTE: With the right hand, partially mute the note by lightly touching the string just before the bridge.

MUFFLED STRINGS: Lay the left hand across the strings without depressing them to the fretboard; strike the strings with the right hand, producing a percussive sound.

PICK SLIDE: Rub the pick edge down the length of the string to produce a scratchy sound.

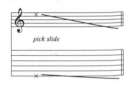

TREMOLO PICKING: Pick the note as rapidly and continuously as possible.

RHYTHM SLASHES: Strum chords in rhythm indicated. Use chord voicings found in the fingering diagrams at the top of the first page of the transcription.

SINGLE-NOTE RHYTHM SLASHES: The circled number above the note name indicates which string to play. When successive notes are played on the same string, only the fret numbers are given.